J. S. BACH'S
ORIGINAL HYMN-TUNES

FOR

CONGREGATIONAL USE

EDITED, WITH NOTES, BY

CHARLES SANFORD TERRY
LITT.D. (CANTAB.), HON. MUS.D. (EDIN.)

Travis & Emery

Charles Sanford Terry:

J. S. Bach's Original Hymn Tunes.

Facsimile of 1922 edition.

First published Oxford University Press 1922.

Republished Travis & Emery 2009.

Published by
Travis & Emery Music Bookshop
17 Cecil Court, London, WC2N 4EZ, United Kingdom.
(+44) 20 7240 2129
neworders@travis-and-emery.com

ISBN Hardback: 978-1-906857-33-2   Paperback: 978-1-906857-34-9

Charles Sanford Terry (1864-1936), Historian and Bach Scholar.

He studied at St. Pauls Cathedral Choir School as a solo boy, King's College and Lancing. He studied history at Cambridge and lectured in history at Durham College of Science and at Aberdeen. He spent much of his life devoted to Music and to Bach in particular. He started choral societies in both Newcastle and Durham. He wrote extensively on Bach. Walter Emery said that his biography of Bach was "the only one that is both detailed and readable". I have a theory that it is easier to read books by musicians who were trained in English or history.

More details available from
- Stanley Sadie: The New Grove Dictionary of Music and Musicians.(Walter Emery).
- Dictionary of National Biography

Works:
Bach's B Minor Mass (1915)
Bach's Chorals (1915-1921, reprint Travis & Emery 2009)
Forkell (Translated C.S.T.): Johann Sebastian Bach: His Life, Art and Work. (1920)
J.S. Bach's Original Hymn-Tunes for Congregational Use (edited by Terry. 1922)
Bach: The Mass in B Minor (1924)
Bach: Coffee and Cupid (edited by C.S. Terry 1924)
Bach: The Cantatas and Oratorios (1925)
Bach: The Passions (1926).
Joh. Seb. Bach: Cantata Texts, sacred and Secular (1926, reprint Travis & Emery 2009)
Bach: a Biography (1928)
Bach: the Magnificat, Lutheran Masses and Motets (1929)
The Four Part Chorals of J.S. Bach (edited C.S.T. 1924, reprint Travis & Emery 2009)
The Origin of the Family of Bach Musicians (1929, reprint Travis & Emery 2009)
John Christian Bach (1929, reprint Travis & Emery 2009)
Bach: the Historical Approach (1930)
Bach's Orchestra (1932)
The Music of Bach (1933)

PRINTED IN ENGLAND
AT THE OXFORD UNIVERSITY PRESS
BY FREDERICK HALL

PREFACE

In the second volume of my 'Bach's Chorals'[1] I considered the Hymn melodies attributed to Bach. Rejecting summarily eighteen tunes ascribed to him by Carl von Winterfeld, Spitta and others, I selected forty-two found in collections or circumstances which made Bach's authorship not improbable. Seven of them are in the 'Notenbüchlein' prepared by Bach for his second wife, Anna Magdalena, in 1725. Twenty-one are in the 'Musicalisches Gesang-Buch' published at Leipzig in 1736 for Georg Christian Schemelli, of which Bach was the musical editor. Three occur in F. W. Birnstiel's edition (Part II, 1769) of Bach's 'Choralgesänge'. One is among the 'Choralgesänge' edited (Part III, 1786) by Bach's second son, Carl Philipp Emmanuel. Two are in C. F. Becker's edition (1843) of the 'Choralgesänge'. Seven tunes are in the MS. of Johann Ludwig Krebs, Bach's pupil, 1726–35. Finally, there are two Choral Arias in the 'Christmas Oratorio' (Nos. 38–40, 42), and one in the Motett 'Komm, Jesu, komm'. The last three are the only tunes of his own composition in his concerted Church music wedded by Bach to the stanzas of a congregational Hymn.

Besides the Oratorio and Motett melodies, I was able to accept thirty of the remaining thirty-nine tunes as being either positively or with practical certainty Bach's original compositions. Of the selected thirty, six are in the 'Notenbüchlein' of 1725, sixteen in Schemelli's Hymn-book, two in Birnstiel's 'Choralgesänge' (1769), one in Part III of the 'Choralgesänge' of 1786, one in Becker's collection (1843), four in Krebs' MS. Twenty-six of these thirty melodies are included in the present volume, the excluded four being—one in the 'Notenbüchlein' ('Gedenke doch, mein Geist, zurücke'), which is an Aria with instrumental interludes; and three in Krebs' MS. ('Gott, mein Herz dir Dank zusendet'; 'Ich gnüge mich an meinem Stande'; 'Meine Seele, lass' es gehen'), of which no bass survives.

---

[1] 'Bach's Chorals: The Hymns and Hymn Melodies of the Cantatas and Motetts' (Cambridge University Press, 1917).

J. S. BACH'S ORIGINAL HYMN-TUNES

Schweitzer has insisted [1] that Bach's Hymn-tunes are sacred Arias rather than Chorals, their peculiar loveliness arising from the fact that they are the work of a composer steeped in the traditions and idiom of the German Choral, but writing under the influence of Italian melodic form. They are practically unknown, though one or two of them have found their way into modern hymn-books, and some of them have been adapted by Dr. W. G. Whittaker [2] to the purpose for which, wrongly, I hold, Schweitzer thought them alone appropriate, namely, as Arias for treble voices.

The chief, I would even say the only, impediment against their English use in the conditions for which Bach designed them is their lack of suitable words. The German originals are in every case of Bach's own period, whose hymnody has characteristics not entirely agreeable to English taste. Moreover, there are practical reasons why new melodies should be wedded to words in common English use. But the German metres are frequently so irregular that the range of appropriate English hymns is considerably restricted, and in four cases (Nos. 6, 17, 19, 21) I have been obliged to fall back upon a translation of the German original. I desire to express my thanks to Mr. Athelstan Riley for his kindness in permitting me to use the words of No. 3, and to the Very Rev. P. L. Carew, Fr. Superior of Mount Saint Bernard's Abbey, for No. 23.

It is interesting to discover the sources whence Bach took the hymns enriched by his melodies. The only hymn-book in his possession at the time of his death was Paul Wagner's 'Andächtiger Seelen geistliches Brand- und Gantz-Opfer' (8 vols., Leipzig, 1697), in use at Leipzig throughout the eighteenth century ; it contained more than five thousand hymns, but no melodies. Among them are Nos. 5, 9, 11, 12, 16, 18, 20, 25 *infra*.

It is exceedingly improbable that Bach was responsible for the selection of the hymns included by Georg Christian Schemelli, Schloss-Cantor at Zeitz, in his 'Musicalisches Gesang-Buch', published by Bernhard Christoph Breitkopf at Leipzig in 1736. The book contains 954 hymns, free from sectarian colouring, an anthology of

---

[1] 'J. S. Bach,' vol. i. 22.   [2] Messrs. Stainer & Bell.

tho treasures of German hymnody, on the model of Johann Anastasius Freylinghausen's popular hymn-book (1704). That the literary
editor of such a book, published at Leipzig by a firm with which
Bach must have been very familiar, should have sought the famous
Cantor's assistance hardly needs further explanation. Spitta,[1] however, supposes that Bach was recommended to Schemelli by the
latter's son, Christian Friedrich, who in the spring of 1735 matriculated
at Leipzig University and eventually succeeded to his father's office
at Zeitz. Schemelli's Preface states that the sixty-nine melodies
printed in the volume had been either composed by Bach or improved
by his addition of a figured bass. Forty-seven of the sixty-nine
melodies Bach took from other hymn-books ; one (No. 23 infra) is
marked by his name as its composer ; the remaining twenty-one
melodies appeared in print for the first time, and sixteen of them
(Nos. 1, 2, 3, 4, 5, 7, 10, 11, 12, 13, 14, 15, 16, 17, 19, 21 infra)
undoubtedly were composed by Bach himself.[2]

Five of the selected melodies are found in the 'Notenbüchlein'
(Nos. 4, 6, 22, 24, 26 infra). Not one of the hymns to which they
are set appears in Wagner's volumes. Nos. 4, 6, and 26, however,
were in general vogue. No. 22 appeared in a hymn-book published
at Dresden in 1725, and therefore within Bach's range of observation.
No. 24, not improbably, is by Bach himself.

The Preface to Schemelli's Hymn-book announced that two hundred
more melodies were ready for a second edition. Among them are
four of Bach's tunes preserved among his detached 'Choralgesänge'
(Nos. 9, 18, 20, 25 infra). The hymns to which he set them he found
in every case in Paul Wagner's volumes. Among the additional
melodies referred to by Schemelli presumably was that of No. 8 infra.
The hymn is tuneless in the 'Musicalisches Gesang-Buch', but
a melody which bears its name survives in the MS. of Krebs,
who was Bach's pupil in 1735, when Schemelli's book was being
prepared.

---

[1] Vol. iii. 109.
[2] The five remaining melodies are : 'Auf, auf, die rechte Zeit ist hier,' 'Ich
liebe Jesum alle Stund,' ' Jesu, deine Liebeswunden,' 'Selig, wer an Jesum
denkt,' ' So wünsch ich mir zu guterlezt.' None of them bears Bach's impress.
See them in my ' Bach's Chorals ', ii. 74 f.

J. S. BACH'S ORIGINAL HYMN-TUNES

I add the following notes on the twenty-six hymns :

1. *Ach, dass nicht die letzte Stunde* (Erdmann Neumeister, 1671–1756). First published, in 6 stanzas, in the 1717 edition of the author's 'Der Zugang zum Gnaden-Stuhl Jesu Christi'. It had no distinctive melody until Bach supplied one (Schemelli). Two years later (1738), Johann Balthasar König (1691–1758) gave it another which had considerable vogue in later hymn-books.

2. *Beschränkt, ihr Weisen dieser Welt* (Christoph Wegleiter, 1659–1706). First published, in 12 stanzas, in the Nürnberg 'Glauben-schallende und Himmel-steigende Herzens-Music' (1703). Cornelius Heinrich Dretzel (1698–1775), five years before Schemelli printed it with Bach's melody, had included it, with four tunes probably by himself, in the Nürnberg 'Des Evangelischen Zions Musicalische Harmonie' (1731).

3. *Dich bet ich an, mein höchster Gott* (Johann Gottfried Olearius, 1635–1711). First published, in 7 stanzas, in the author's 'Tägliches Bet-Lied' (Halle: 1686). Bach's (Schemelli) was its first distinctive melody.

4. *Dir, dir, Jehovah, will ich singen* (Bartholomäus Crasselius, 1667–1724). First published, in 8 stanzas, in the Halle 'Geistreiches Gesangbuch' (1697), and, to an anonymous melody, in the Darmstadt 'Geistreiches Gesang-Buch' of 1698. The hymn is widely known and has received several melodies besides Bach's (Schemelli). Translations are noted in the 'Dictionary of Hymnology', p. 268.

5. *Eins ist noth, ach Herr, dies eine* (Johann Heinrich Schröder, 1667–99). First published, in 10 stanzas, in the Halle 'Geistreiches Gesangbuch' (1697). The hymn has received several melodies besides Bach's (Schemelli). Translations are noted in the 'Dictionary of Hymnology', p. 1016.

6. *Gieb dich zufrieden und sei stille* (Paul Gerhardt, 1607–76). First published, in 15 stanzas, in its author's 'Geistliche Andachten' (Berlin: 1666) to a melody (engraved in Winterfeld's 'Der Evangelische Kirchengesang', ii. No. 97) by Johann Georg Ebeling (1637–76). Two other melodies

6

to which it was sung are found, one of them his own, in Bach's 'Notenbüchlein' (1725). The other is not known in print earlier than König's compilation (1738) (see No. 1 *supra*). Zahn, 'Die Melodien der deutschen evangelischen Kirchenlieder' (No. 7419), is disposed to attribute it to König himself. Its earlier existence in Bach's MS. forbids that conclusion ; but the tune is certainly not by Bach.

7. *Gott, wie gross ist deine Güte* (Georg Christian Schemelli, b. 1676). First printed, in 4 stanzas with Bach's melody, in the 'Musicalisches Gesang-Buch' (Leipzig: 1736).

8. *Hier lieg ich nun, O Vater aller Gnaden* (Johann Arndt, 1555–1621). Printed, in 6 stanzas without a melody, in Schemelli, who quotes it from the author's 'Paradiss-Gärtlein' (1612).

9. *Ich bin ja, Herr, in deiner Macht* (Simon Dach, 1605–59). First printed, in 8 stanzas, in its author's 'Christliche Todes-Errinnerung' (Königsberg: 1648) to a melody by Heinrich Albert (1604–51) (in Winterfeld, ii. No. 68). Zahn (Nos. 5869a–5878b) prints ten melodies to which the popular hymn has been sung.

10. *Ich halte treulich still.* First printed, in 12 stanzas, in Schemelli (1736), with Bach's melody. Schemelli attributes it to 'J. H. Till', of whom nothing is known, unless he is identified with Jakob T. Till (1713–83).

11. *Ich steh an deiner Krippen hier* (Paul Gerhardt, 1607–76). First printed, in 15 stanzas, in Johann Crüger's 'Praxis Pietatis Melica' (Berlin : 1653). It already possessed four melodies before Bach (Schemelli) added another.

12. *Jesu, Jesu, du bist mein.* First printed, in 8 stanzas, in the Darmstadt 'Cantional' (1687). Bach's melody (Schemelli) is one of several associated with the. hymn. Hardenberg's MS. Liederlexikon at Wernigerode names Caspar Zollikofer (1707–79) as the author.

13. *Komm, süsser Tod.* First printed, in 10 stanzas, in the Dresden 'Gesangbuch' (1725). Bach's (Schemelli) melody is one of several associated with it. Hardenberg's MS. (see No. 12

supra) names Johann Christian Dieterich (1712–1800) as the author.

14. *Kommt, Seelen, dieser Tag* (Valentin Ernst Löscher, 1673–1749). First printed, in 7 stanzas, in the author's 'Dreifache Andachtsübung' (Dresden: 1713). Schemelli directs it to be sung, in alternate stanzas, with another Whitsuntide hymn, 'Komm, Gott Schöpfer, heiliger Geist'.

15. *Kommt wieder aus der finstern Gruft* (Valentin Ernst Löscher, 1673–1749). First printed, in 7 stanzas, in the author's 'Dreifache Andachtsübung' (Dresden: 1713). In Schemelli it is directed to be sung, in alternate stanzas, with the Easter 'Heut triumphiret Gottes Sohn'. See No. 14 *supra*.

16. *Liebster Herr Jesu, wo bleibst du so lange?* The hymn is attributed both to Christoph Werner (fl. 1655) and Christoph Weselovius. Of the latter nothing is known. He may perhaps be identified with the Christoph Weselohe, or Weseloph, who represented Osnabrück at the Regensburg Diet in 1684 (J. H. Zedler's 'Grosses Universal-Lexikon' (Leipzig and Halle, 1748, vol. lv, col. 739). Set to a melody by Heinrich Schwemmer (1621–96), it is found, in 7 stanzas, in the Nürnberg 'Gesang-Buch' (1676).

17. *Mein Jesu, was vor Seelenweh* (Georg Christian Schemelli, b. 1676). First printed, in 6 stanzas, in the author's 'Musicalisches Gesang-Buch' (1736) with Bach's melody. The metre is that of the familiar 'Wie schön leuchtet der Morgenstern'. See Nos. 14 and 15 *supra*.

18. *Nicht so traurig, nicht so sehr* (Paul Gerhardt, 1607–76). First printed, in 15 stanzas, in Johann Crüger's 'Praxis Pietatis Melica' (Berlin: 1647). Crüger (1598–1662) gave it a melody (Winterfeld, ii. No. 80) which is still in common use. Bach's ('Choralgesänge,' 1769) is one of twenty-five settings of the popular hymn printed by Zahn (Nos. 3336–3363).

19. *O finstre Nacht, wann wirst du doch vergehen?* (Georg Friedrich Breithaupt, fl. 1700). First printed, in 10 stanzas, in Johann Anastasius Freylinghausen's 'Geistreiches Gesang-Buch' (Halle: 1704). Ludwig Steiner (1688–1761) had already

provided it with a melody in his 'Neues Gesang-Buch' (Zürich : 1723) before Bach gave it another (Schemelli). The author was Secretarius at Laubach.

20. *O Herzensangst, O Bangigkeit und Zagen* (Fr. D. Gerh. Müller). The hymn, in 9 stanzas, is in the ninth edition of the Breslau 'Vollständige Kirchen- und Haus-Music' (1700), and probably is of earlier date. The author, or authoress, is described by Zahn (No. 1003) as 'von Königsberg', where, however, his or her memory has not survived. Bach's melody ('Choralgesänge,' 1769) is found in a few nineteenth-century hymnbooks.

21. *O liebe Seele, zieh die Sinnen* (Anon.). First printed, in 12 stanzas, and with Bach's melody, in Schemelli (1736). Not improbably it is by Schemelli himself.

22. *Schaffs mit mir, Gott, nach deinem Willen* (Benjamin Schmolck, 1672–1737). First printed, in 11 stanzas, in the Dresden 'Gesangbuch' (1725) (see No. 13 *supra*). The initial letters of its stanzas give the acrostic 'S. R. Zieroldin', in memory of whom presumably it was written.[1] Bach's (its only) melody ('Notenbüchlein,' 1725) passed into the hymn-books (Zahn, No. 2883).

23. *Vergiss mein nicht, mein allerliebster Gott* (Anon.). First printed, in 5 stanzas, with Bach's melody, in Schemelli (1736). Not improbably it is by Schemelli himself.

24. *Warum betrübst du dich, Und beugest?* (Anon.). A single stanza, with the melody, is in the 'Notenbüchlein' (1725). The stanza is not found before 1725, and probably Bach wrote it.

25. *Was betrübst du dich, mein Herze?* (Zacharias Hermann, 1643–1716). Is included, in 12 stanzas, and without a melody, in the author's 'Frommer Christen Seuffzende Seele und Singender Mund' (Breslau and Leipzig : 1722). In Paul Wagner's Leipzig Hymn-book (vol. vi, 152) it is directed to be sung to Johann Schop's (d. c. 1665) melody 'Werde

---

[1] So I am informed by the Rev. James Mearns, to whose unique knowledge of German hymnody I am generally indebted.

J. S. BACH'S ORIGINAL HYMN-TUNES

munter, mein Gemüthe'. Bach's ('Choralgesänge,' 1843) did not find its way into the hymn-books.

26. *Wie wohl ist mir, O Freund der Seelen* (Wolfgang Christoph Dessler, 1660–1722). First printed, in 6 stanzas, and with a melody by Benedikt Schultheiss (d. 1693), in the author's 'Gott-geheiligter Christen nützlich-ergetzende Seelen-Lust' (Nürnberg: 1692). Zahn (Nos. 7791–7800) prints nine others besides Bach's ('Notenbüchlein,' 1725).

The following Table states the original key of the twenty-six melodies, the condition of their original bass, and source:

No.	Original key.	Bass.	Source.
1.	E mi.	Figured	Schemelli, No. 831.
2.	A ma.	,,	,, No. 689.
3.	D ma.	,,	,, No. 396.
4.	B flat ma.	Unfigured	'Notenbüchlein,' p. 51.
	,,	Score	B.G. xxxix, No. 46.
	,,	*Another Bass (Figured)	Schemelli, No. 397 (Erk, 'Choralgesänge,' No. 20).
5.	C ma.	Figured	Schemelli, No. 112.
6.	G mi.	*Unfigured	'Notenbüchlein,' p. 31.
	E mi.	Unfigured (slightly different Bass)	,, p. 31 (Erk, No. 208; Richter, 'Choralgesänge,' No. 111).
7.	B flat ma.	Figured	Schemelli, No. 360.
8.	F mi.	Unfigured	Krebs MS.
9.	G mi.	Score	B.G. xxxix, No. 92.
10.	F ma.	Figured	Schemelli, No. 657.
11.	C mi.	,,	,, No. 195.
12.	C mi.	,,	,, No. 741.
	,,	Score	B.G. xxxix, No. 104.
13.	,,	Figured	Schemelli, No. 868.
14.	F ma.	,,	,, No. 936.
15.	A ma.	,,	,, No. 938.
16.	G mi.	,,	,, No. 874.
17.	D mi.	,,	,, No. 283.
18.	C mi.	Score	B.G. xxxix, No. 131.
19.	B mi.	Figured	Schemelli, No. 891.
20.	E flat ma.	Score	B.G. xxxix, No. 147.
21.	G ma.	Figured	Schemelli, No. 575.
22.	C ma.	,,	'Notenbüchlein,' p. 48.
23.	A mi.	Unfigured	Schemelli, No. 627.
24.	F mi.	,,	'Notenbüchlein,' p. 46.
25.	G mi.	Score	B.G. xxxix, No. 170.
26.	F ma.	Unfigured	'Notenbüchlein,' p. 51.

* These versions are not followed in this collection.

10

FOR CONGREGATIONAL USE

I acknowledge my obligation to Dr. W. G. Whittaker, who has read the proofs of the music texts and confirmed or corrected my interpretation of Bach's figuring.

The words to which the melodies are set in this collection, with the few exceptions already remarked, are in common use in the official Hymn-books of the Episcopal and Presbyterian Churches of these kingdoms. (See Index of First Lines.)

C. SANFORD TERRY.

KING'S COLLEGE,
OLD ABERDEEN.
February, 1922.

CONTENTS

1

(For General Use)

Moderately slow ♩ = 60.

Bishop W. W. How, 1823–97.

WHO is this so weak and helpless,
  Child of lowly Hebrew maid,
Rudely in a stable sheltered,
  Coldly in a manger laid?
'Tis the Lord of all creation,
  Who this wondrous path hath trod;
He is God from everlasting,
  And to everlasting God.

2 Who is this—a Man of Sorrows,
  Walking sadly life's hard way,
Homeless, weary, sighing, weeping
  Over sin and Satan's sway?

'Tis our God, our glorious Saviour,
  Who above the starry sky
Now for us a place prepareth
  Where no tear can dim the eye.

3 Who is this—behold Him raining
  Drops of blood upon the ground?
Who is this—despised, rejected,
  Mocked, insulted, beaten, bound?
'Tis our God, who gifts and graces
  On his Church now poureth down;
Who shall smite in holy vengeance
  All his foes beneath his throne.

4. Who is this that hangeth dying,
    With the thieves on either side?
Nails his hands and feet are tearing,
    And the spear hath pierced his side.
  'Tis the God who ever liveth
    'Mid the shining ones on high,
  In the glorious golden city
    Reigning everlastingly.

A-men.

13

J. S. BACH'S ORIGINAL HYMN-TUNES

2

(For General Use)

In moderate time ♩ = 80.

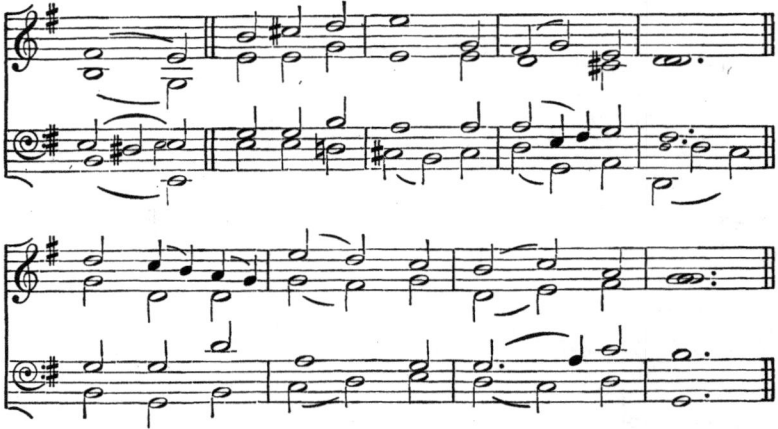

Francis T. Palgrave, 1824–97.

THRICE-HOLY Name! that sweeter sounds
   Than streams which down the valley run,
And tells of more than human love,
   And more than human power, in one :
First from the gracious herald heard,
   Heard since through all the choirs on high ;
O Child of Mary, Son of God,
   Eternal, hear thy children's cry !
     While at the blessèd Name we bow,
     Lord Jesus, be among us now!

2 Within our dim-eyed souls call up
   The vision of thine earthly years ;
The Mount of thy transfigured Form ;
   The Garden of thy bitter Tears ;
The Cross upreared in darkening skies ;
   The thorn-wreathed Head, the bleeding Side ;
And whisper in the heart, 'For you,
   For you, I left the heavens, and died.'
     While at the blessèd Name we bow,
     Lord Jesus, be among us now!

3. Ah ! with faith's inward piercing eye
   The rivèn rock-hewn bed we see,
Whence thou in triumph hast gone forth
   By death from death to make us free !
And when on earth's last awful day
   The Judgement-seat of God shall shine,
Lift thou our trembling eyes to read
   In thy dear Face the mercy-sign.
     While at the blessèd Name we bow,
     Lord Jesus, be among us now.

A-men.

15

J. S. BACH'S ORIGINAL HYMN-TUNES

3

(For General Use)

FOR CONGREGATIONAL USE

Athelstan Riley, 1858–

YE watchers and ye holy ones,
Bright Seraphs, Cherubim and Thrones,
Raise the glad strain, Alleluya!
Cry out, Dominions, Princedoms, Powers,
Virtues, Archangels, Angels' choirs, Alleluya!
Alleluya, Alleluya, Alleluya!

2 O higher than the Cherubim,
More glorious than the Seraphim,
Lead their praises, Alleluya!
Thou Bearer of the eternal Word,
Most gracious, magnify the Lord, Alleluya!
●*Alleluya, Alleluya, Alleluya!*

3 Respond, ye souls in endless rest,
Ye Patriarchs and Prophets blest,
Alleluya, Alleluya!
Ye holy Twelve, ye Martyrs strong,
All Saints triumphant, raise the song, Alleluya!
Alleluya, Alleluya, Alleluya!

4. O friends, in gladness let us sing,
Supernal anthems echoing,
Alleluya, Alleluya!
To God the Father, God the Son,
And God the Spirit, Three in One, Alleluya!
Alleluya, Alleluya, Alleluya!

A-men.

B

4

(For General Use or Almsgiving)

In moderate time ♩ = 84.

FOR CONGREGATIONAL USE

Bishop Christopher Wordsworth, 1807–85.

O LORD of heav'n, and earth, and sea,
  To thee all praise and glory be ;
How shall we show our love to thee,
      Who givest all ? *(bis)*

2 The golden sunshine, vernal air,
  Sweet flowers and fruits, thy love declare ;
  When harvests ripen, thou art there,
      Who givest all. *(bis)*

3 For peaceful homes, and healthful days,
  For all the blessings earth displays,
  We owe thee thankfulness and praise,
      Who givest all. *(bis)*

4 Thou didst not spare thine only Son,
  But gav'st him for a world undone,
  And freely with that Blessèd One
      Thou givest all. *(bis)*

5 Thou giv'st the Holy Spirit's dower,
  Spirit of life, and love, and power,
  And dost his sevenfold graces shower
      Upon us all. *(bis)*

6 For souls redeemed, for sins forgiven,
  For means of grace and hopes of Heaven,
  Father, what can to thee be given,
      Who givest all ? *(bis)*

7 We lose what on ourselves we spend,
  We have as treasure without end
  Whatever, Lord, to thee we lend,
      Who givest all ; *(bis)*

8. To thee, from whom we all derive
  Our life, our gifts, our power to give :
  O may we ever with thee live,
      Who givest all. *(bis)*

A-men.

5

(For Eastertide)

FOR CONGREGATIONAL USE

Bishop Christopher Wordsworth, 1807–85.
With Refrain by C. S. T.

ALLELUYA! Alleluya!
Hearts to heaven and voices raise;
Sing to God a hymn of gladness,
Sing to God a hymn of praise;

Alleluya! Alleluya! Christ Jesus is risen!
O come all ye faithful and raise your acclaim;
For burst are the bars of Hell's powerless prison,
And Death is the captive of him who was slain.

2 Christ is risen, Christ the first-fruits
Of the holy harvest field,
Which will all its full abundance
At his second coming yield;

Alleluya! Alleluya! Christ Jesus is risen!
O come all ye faithful and raise your acclaim;
For burst are the bars of Hell's powerless prison,
And Death is the captive of him who was slain.

3 Christ is risen, we are risen;
Shed upon us heavenly grace,
Rain, and dew, and gleams of glory
From the brightness of thy face;

Alleluya! Alleluya! Christ Jesus is risen!
O come all ye faithful and raise your acclaim;
For burst are the bars of Hell's powerless prison,
And Death is the captive of him who was slain.

4. Alleluya! Alleluya!
Glory be to God on high;
To the Father, and the Saviour,
Who has gain'd the victory;

Alleluya! Alleluya! Christ Jesus is risen!
O come all ye faithful and raise your acclaim;
For burst are the bars of Hell's powerless prison,
And Death is the captive of him who was slain.

A-men.

6

(For General Use)

Rather slow $\quad \downarrow = 54.$

FOR CONGREGATIONAL USE

Paul Gerhardt, 1607–76.
Tr. Anon.

O PRAISE the God of our salvation,
Trust him ever who hath made us.
He is the hope of every nation,
Never shall his mercy fail us!
He is our Source, our Sun, Life-giver,
He lights us on our pathway ever.
Be thou content, he will not fail!

2 He hears our sighs and knows our sorrows,
Listens to our timid pleading.
The faintest heart his guidance borrows,
Though it knows not what 'tis needing.
He stands before us, ever loving,
His arms of welcome ever opening.
Be thou content, he will not fail!

3. One day we shall in heaven meet him,
He our joy and consolation,
With souls elect we there shall greet him,
Saved from death and desolation,
In his dread sight for ever standing,
With him in fullest understanding.
Be thou content, he will not fail!

A-men.

7

(For General Use)

FOR CONGREGATIONAL USE

Charles Wesley, 1707-88.

LOVE Divine, all loves excelling,
    Joy of heaven, to earth come down,
Fix in us thy humble dwelling,
    All thy faithful mercies crown.
Jesu, thou art all compassion,
    Pure unbounded love thou art ;
Visit us with thy salvation,
    Enter every trembling heart.

2 Come, almighty to deliver,
    Let us all thy life receive ;
Suddenly return, and never,
    Never more thy temples leave.
Thee we would be always blessing,
    Serve thee as thy hosts above,
Pray, and praise thee, without ceasing,
    Glory in thy perfect love.

3. Finish then thy new creation,
    Pure and spotless let us be ;
Let us see thy great salvation,
    Perfectly restored in thee,
Changed from glory into glory,
    Till in heaven we take our place,
Till we cast our crowns before thee,
    Lost in wonder, love, and praise !

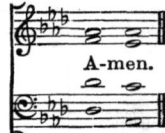

A-men.

8

(Holy Communion)

FOR CONGREGATIONAL USE

St. Thomas Aquinas, 1227-74.
Tr. Bishop J. R. Woodford.

THEE we adore, O hidden Saviour, thee,
Who in thy Sacrament art pleased to be ;
Both flesh and spirit in thy presence fail,
Yet here thy Presence we devoutly hail.

2 O blest Memorial of our dying Lord,
Who living Bread to men doth here afford !
O may our souls for ever feed on thee,
And thou, O Christ, for ever precious be.

3 Fountain of goodness, Jesu, Lord and God,
Cleanse us, unclean, with thy most cleansing Blood ;
Increase our faith and love, that we may know
The hope and peace which from thy Presence flow.

4. O Christ, whom now beneath a veil we see,
May what we thirst for soon our portion be,
To gaze on thee unveiled, and see thy face,
The vision of thy glory and thy grace.

A-men.

9

(For General Use)

In moderate time ♩ = 60.

FOR CONGREGATIONAL USE

Bishop Reginald Heber, **1783-1826.**

HOSANNA to the living Lord!
Hosanna to the Incarnate Word!
To Christ, Creator, Saviour, King,
Let earth, let heaven Hosanna sing,
Hosanna in the highest!

2 O Saviour, with protecting care
Abide in this thy house of prayer,
Where we thy parting promise claim,
Assembled in thy sacred Name.
Hosanna in the highest!

3 But, chiefest, in our cleansèd breast,
Eternal, bid thy Spirit rest;
And make our secret soul to be
A temple pure and worthy thee.
Hosanna in the highest!

4. To God the Father, God the Son,
And God the Spirit, Three in One,
Be honour, praise, and glory given
By all on earth and all in heaven.
Hosanna in the highest!

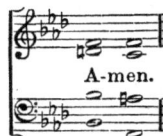

A-men.

10

(For General Use)

FOR CONGREGATIONAL USE

Charles Wesley, 1707–88.

COMMIT thou all thy griefs
   And ways into his hands,
To his sure truth and tender care,
   Who earth and heaven commands,
   Who points the clouds their course,
   Whom winds and seas obey ;
He shall direct thy wandering feet,
   He shall prepare thy way.

2   Thou on the Lord rely,
      So safe shalt thou go on ;
   Fix on his work thy steadfast eye,
      So shall thy work be done.
      Give to the winds thy fears ;
      Hope, and be undismayed ;
   God hears thy sighs and counts thy tears ;
      God shall lift up thy head.

3.   Through waves and clouds and storms
       He gently clears thy way ;
    Wait thou his time ; so shall this night
       Soon end in joyous day.
       Leave to his sovereign sway
       To choose and to command ;
    So shalt thou, wondering, own his way
       How wise, how strong his hand.

A-men.

11

(Passiontide)

Slow and dignified ♩ = 56.

FOR CONGREGATIONAL USE

Attolle paulum lumina, c. 17th century.
Tr. John Mason Neale.

O SINNER, raise the eye of faith,
  To true repentance turning,
Consider well the curse of sin,
  Its shame and guilt discerning:
Upon the Crucified One look,
So shalt thou learn, as in a book,
  What well is worth thy learning.

2 Look on the head, with such a crown
  Of bitter thorns surrounded;
Look on the blood that trickles down
  The feet and hands thus wounded;
And see his flesh with scourges rent:
Mark how upon the Innocent
  Man's malice hath abounded.

3 But though upon him many a pain
  Its bitterness is spending,
Yet more, O how much more! his heart
  Man's wickedness is rending!
Such is the load for sinners borne,
As Mary's Son in woe forlorn
  His life for us is ending.

4 None ever knew such pangs before,
  None ever such affliction,
As when his people brought to pass
  The Saviour's crucifixion.
He willed to bear for us the throes,
For us the unimagined woes,
  Of death's most fell infliction.

5 O sinner, stay and ponder well
  Sin's fearful condemnation;
Think on the wounds that Christ endured
  In working thy salvation;
For if thy Lord had never died,
Nought else could sinful man betide
  But utter reprobation.

6. Lord, give us sinners grace to flee
  The death of evil-doing,
To shun the gloomy gates of hell,
  Thine awful judgement viewing.
So thank we thee, O Christ, to-day,
And so for life eternal pray,
  The holy road pursuing.

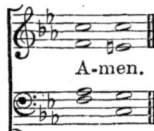

A-men.

33

12

(For General Use)

FOR CONGREGATIONAL USE

Charles Wesley, 1707–88.

JESU, Lover of my soul,
  Let me to thy bosom fly,
While the nearer waters roll,
  While the tempest still is high :
Hide me, O my Saviour, hide,
  Till the storm of life is past ;
Safe into the haven guide,
  O receive my soul at last.

2 Other refuge have I none ;
  Hangs my helpless soul on thee ;
Leave, ah ! leave me not alone,
  Still support and comfort me.
All my trust on thee is stayed,
  All my help from thee I bring ;
Cover my defenceless head
  With the shadow of thy wing.

3 Thou, O Christ, art all I want ;
  More than all in thee I find :
Raise the fallen, cheer the faint,
  Heal the sick, and lead the blind.
Just and holy is thy name ;
  I am all unrighteousness ;
False and full of sin I am,
  Thou art full of truth and grace.

4. Plenteous grace with thee is found,
  Grace to cover all my sin ;
Let the healing streams abound ;
  Make and keep me pure within.
Thou of life the fountain art ;
  Freely let me take of thee ;
Spring thou up within my heart,
  Rise to all eternity.

A-men.

13

(For General Use)

FOR CONGREGATIONAL USE

Frederick William Faber, **1814–63.** *

O PARADISE ! O Paradise !
    Who doth not crave for rest ?
Who would not seek the happy land
    Where they that loved are blest ?
      Where loyal hearts and true
      Stand ever in the light,
      In God's most holy sight.

2 O Paradise ! O Paradise !
    The world is growing old ;
Who would not be at rest and free
    Where love is never cold ?
      Where loyal hearts and true
      Stand ever in the light,
      In God's most holy sight.

3 O Paradise ! O Paradise !
    'Tis weary waiting here ;
I long to be where Jesus is,
    To feel, to see him near ;
      Where loyal hearts and true
      Stand ever in the light,
      In God's most holy sight.

4 O Paradise ! O Paradise !
    I want to sin no more,
I want to be as pure on earth
    As on thy spotless shore ;
      Where loyal hearts and true
      Stand ever in the light,
      In God's most holy sight.

5 O Paradise ! O Paradise !
    I greatly long to see
The special place my dearest Lord
    In love prepares for me ;
      Where loyal hearts and true
      Stand ever in the light.
      In God's most holy sight.

6. Lord Jesu, King of Paradise,
    O keep me in thy love,
And guide me to that happy land
    Of perfect rest above ;
      Where loyal hearts and true
      Stand ever in the light,
      In God's most holy sight.

A-men.

* The seventh line of each stanza is omitted.

14

(Thanksgiving)

In moderate time ♩ = 96.

FOR CONGREGATIONAL USE

Martin Rinkart, 1586–1649.
Tr. Catherine Winkworth.

NOW thank we all our God,
With heart and hands and voices,
Who wondrous things hath done,
In whom his world rejoices;
Who from our mother's arms
Hath blessed us on our way
With countless gifts of love,
And still is ours to-day.

2 O may this bounteous God
Through all our life be near us,
With ever joyful hearts
And blessèd peace to cheer us;
And keep us in his grace,
And guide us when perplexed,
And free us from all ills
In this world and the next.

3. All praise and thanks to God
The Father now be given,
The Son, and him who reigns
With them in highest heaven,
The One eternal God,
Whom earth and heaven adore;
For thus it was, is now,
And shall be evermore.

A-men.

15

(For General Use)

With breadth, but not too slow ♩ = 80.

FOR CONGREGATIONAL USE

J. J. Schütz, 1640–90.
Tr. Frances E. Cox.

SING praise to God who reigns above,
  The God of all creation,
The God of power, the God of love,
  The God of our salvation ;
With healing balm my soul he fills,
And every faithless murmur stills :
  To God all praise and glory !

2 The Angel-host, O King of kings,
  Thy praise for ever telling,
In earth and sky all living things
  Beneath thy shadow dwelling,
Adore the wisdom which could span
And power which formed creation's plan :
  To God all praise and glory !

3 What God's almighty power hath made
  His gracious mercy keepeth ;
By morning glow or evening shade
  His watchful eye ne'er sleepeth :
Within the kingdom of his might
Lo ! all is just, and all is right :
  To God all praise and glory !

4 Then all my gladsome way along
  I sing aloud thy praises,
That men may hear the grateful song
  My voice unwearied raises :
Be joyful in the Lord, my heart !
Both soul and body bear your part !
  To God all praise and glory !

5. O ye who name Christ's holy name,
  Give God all praise and glory :
All ye who own his power, proclaim
  Aloud the wondrous story !
Cast each false idol from his throne,
The Lord is God, and he alone :
  To God all praise and glory !

A-men.

41

16

(Holy Communion)

Moderately slow ♩ = 63.

Ave verum Corpus natum, **14th century.**
Tr. H. N. Oxenham.

HAIL, true Body, born of Mary,
Spotless Virgin's virgin birth;
Thou who truly hangedst weary
On the Cross for sons of earth;
O most kind! O gracious One!
O sweetest Jesu, Mary's most holy Son!

2. Thou whose sacred side was riven,
Whence the Water flowed and Blood,
O mayst thou, dear Lord, be given
At death's hour to be my food:
O most kind! O gracious One!
O sweetest Jesu, Mary's most holy Son!

A-men.

17

(Passiontide)

FOR CONGREGATIONAL USE

Georg Christian Schemelli (b. 1676).
Tr. Anon.

LORD JESUS, bitter was the woe
Befell thee in Gethsemane,
Where wicked men did take thee ;
The pangs of death, the gloom of hell,
Such anguish as no man can tell
Did like a flood o'ertake thee.
What pain, what grief,
Wracked thee 'fore thy Father bending,
Silent and alone,
As thy soul sped, heaven wending.

2. Lord Jesus, finished is the fight,
Thy Body's in its rocky bed,
Thy soul's to God commended.
E'en to the last our sorrow's load
Thou bearest in thine arms to God
Into the clouds ascended.
O hear me, Lord !
Save me in my mortal anguish !
When death bids me come !
Suffer not my soul to languish !

A-men.

18

(*Epiphany*)

FOR CONGREGATIONAL USE

W. Chatterton Dix, 1887–98.

AS with gladness men of old
Did the guiding star behold,
As with joy they hailed its light,
Leading onward, beaming bright,
So, most gracious God, may we
Evermore be led to thee.

2 As with joyful steps they sped
To that lowly manger-bed,
There to bend the knee before
Him whom heaven and earth adore,
So may we with willing feet
Ever seek thy mercy-seat.

3 As they offered gifts most rare
At that manger rude and bare,
So may we with holy joy,
Pure, and free from sin's alloy,
All our costliest treasures bring,
Christ, to thee our heavenly King.

4 Holy Jesu, every day
Keep us in the narrow way ;
And, when earthly things are past,
Bring our ransomed souls at last
Where they need no star to guide,
Where no clouds thy glory hide.

5. In the heavenly country bright
Need they no created light ;
Thou its Light, its Joy, its Crown,
Thou its Sun which goes not down :
There for ever may we sing
Alleluyas to our King.

A-men.

19

(For General Use)

Moderately slow ♩ = 60.

FOR CONGREGATIONAL USE

Georg Friedrich Breithaupt (*fl.* 1700).
Tr. Anon.

O GLOOM of sin, when, when wilt thou pass over?
　　When comes the Light of Life to me?
When shall my feeble earth-bound sight discover
　　The radiant dawn of ecstasy?
When, standing at his judgement-seat,
My God eternally to meet,
And so at peace to rise forgiven
And pass within the gate of heaven?

2. O peaceful death, thou haven long desirèd,
　　When shall I meet thee close at hand?
When shall I shed this body frail and mirèd
　　And in the halls of glory stand?
By God's good grace the fight is won,
And Satan's power is all undone.
Sun of my soul, 'tis thou wilt light me
To thine eternal company.

A-men.

20

(For General Use)

In moderate time ♩ = 69.

FOR CONGREGATIONAL USE

Philip Pusey, 1799–1855.

LORD of our life, and God of our salvation,
Star of our night, and Hope of our nation,
Hear and receive thy Church's supplication,
    Lord God Almighty.

2 See round thine ark the hungry billows curling;
See now thy foes their banners unfurling;
Lord, while their darts envenomed they are hurling,
    Thou canst preserve us.

3 Lord, thou canst help when earthly armour faileth,
Lord, thou canst save us when sin assaileth;
Christ, o'er thy Rock nor death nor hell prevaileth;
    Grant us thy peace, Lord.

4 Peace in our hearts, our evil thoughts assuaging;
Peace in thy Church, where sons are engaging;
Peace, when the world its busy war is waging:
    Calm thy foes' raging.

5. Grant us thy help till backward they are driven,
Grant them thy truth, that they be forgiven;
Grant peace on earth, and, after we have striven,
    Peace in thy heaven.

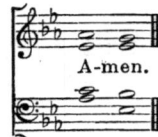

A-men.

21

(For General Use)

FOR CONGREGATIONAL USE

Joachim Magdeburg, c. 1525–88.
Tr. Catherine Winkworth.

WHO puts his trust in God most just
 Hath built his house secure and fast;
He who relies on Jesus Christ
 Shall reach his haven-home at last.
While mine thou art not death's worst smart my soul shall harm
 Nor let my courage fainting be;
 For thy truth stands and e'er shall comfort me.

2 Though fiercest foes my course oppose,
 A dauntless front to them I'll show;
My champion thou, Lord Christ, art now,
 Who soon shall Satan overthrow!
No powers of death nor hell's foul breath shall do me hurt.
 Before thy might my foes disperse;
 'Tis thou dispel'st the shadow of man's curse.

3. I rest me here without a fear,
 By thee shall grace be given free,
And all I need, O Friend indeed,
 For this life or the heavenly.
Lord, hear my prayer, and in thy care vouchsafed to me
 Keep me in peace for evermore
 And grace impart from out thy plenteous store.

A-men.

22

(St. Michael and All Angels)

FOR CONGREGATIONAL USE

St. Joseph the Hymnographer, d. 883.
Tr. J. M. Neale.

STARS of the morning, so gloriously bright,
Filled with celestial resplendence and light,
These that, where night never followeth day,
Raise the Trisagion ever and ay :

2 These are thy counsellors, these dost thou own,
Lord God of Sabaoth, nearest thy throne ;
These are thy ministers, these dost thou send,
Help of the helpless ones ! man to defend.

3 These keep the guard amid Salem's dear bowers ;
Thrones, Principalities, Virtues, and Powers ;
Where, with the Living Ones, mystical Four,
Cherubim, Seraphim bow and adore.

4 'Who like the Lord ?' thunders Michael the Chief ;
Raphael, 'the cure of God,' comforteth grief ;
And, as at Nazareth, prophet of peace,
Gabriel, 'the Light of God,' bringeth release.

5 Then, when the earth was first poised in mid space,
Then, when the planets first sped on their race,
Then, when were ended the six days' employ,
Then all the Sons of God shouted for joy.

6. Still let them succour us ; still let them fight,
Lord of angelic hosts, battling for right ;
Till, where their anthems they ceaselessly pour,
We with the Angels may bow and adore.

A-men.

55

23

(For General Use)

FOR CONGREGATIONAL USE

Henry Collins, 1794–1870
(*slightly altered* *).

JESU, my Lord, *Jesu*, my God, *Jesu*, my All,
Hear me, blest Saviour, when I call ;
Hear me, and from thy dwelling-place
Pour down the riches of thy grace :
　　Jesu, my Lord, I thee adore,
　　O make me love thee *ever* more and more.

2 Jesu, too late, *alas ! too late*, I thee have sought,
How can I love thee as I ought ?
And how extol thy matchless fame,
The glorious beauty of thy name ?
　　Jesu, my Lord, I thee adore,
　　O make me love thee *ever* more and more.

3 Jesu, what *worth* didst *thy compassion* find in me
That thou hast dealt so lovingly ?
How great the joy that thou hast brought,
So far exceeding hope or thought !
　　Jesu, my Lord, I thee adore,
　　O make me love thee *ever* more and more.

4. Jesu, of thee, *always of thee*, shall be my song,
To thee my heart and soul belong ;
All that I am or have is thine,
And thou, sweet Saviour, thou art mine.
　　Jesu, my Lord, I thee adore,
　　O make me love thee *ever* more and more.

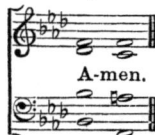

A-men.

* The alterations, made with permission, are additions to the original stanzas necessitated by the metre of the melody.　They are printed in italics.

24

(For General Use)

Sir H. W. Baker, 1821–77.*

THERE is a blessèd home
    Beyond this land of *sin and* woe,
Where trials never come,
    Nor tears of sorrow flow ;
Where faith is lost in sight,
    And patient hope is crowned,
And everlasting light
    Its glory throws around.

2 There is a land of peace,
    Good Angels know *and love* it well,
Glad songs that never cease
    Within its portals swell ;
Around its glorious throne
    Ten thousand Saints adore
Christ, with the Father One
    And Spirit, evermore.

3 O joy all joys beyond,
    To see the Lamb *above* who died,
And count each sacred wound
    In hands, and feet, and side ;
To give to him the praise
    Of every triumph won,
And sing through endless days
    The great things he hath done.

4. Look up, ye saints of God,
    Nor fear to tread *on earth* below
The path your Saviour trod
    Of daily toil and woe ;
Wait but a little while
    In uncomplaining love,
His own most gracious smile
    Shåll welcome you above.

A-men.

* Additions to the original stanzas are printed in italics.

25

(Saints' Days)

Bishop Christopher Wordsworth, 1807–85.

HARK ! the sound of holy voices,
  Chanting at the crystal sea,
Alleluya, Alleluya,
  Alleluya, Lord, to thee :
Multitude, which none can number,
  Like the stars in glory stands,
Clothed in white apparel, holding
  Palms of victory in their hands.

2 Patriarch, and holy Prophet,
  Who prepared the way of Christ,
King, Apostle, Saint, Confessor,
  Martyr, and Evangelist,
Saintly Maiden, godly Matron,
  Widows who have watched to prayer,
Joined in holy concert, singing
  To the Lord of all, are there.

3 They have come from tribulation,
  And have washed their robes in blood,
Washed them in the blood of Jesus ;
  Tried they were, and firm they stood ;
Mocked, imprisoned, stoned, tormented,
  Sawn asunder, slain with sword,
They have conquered death and Satan
  By the might of Christ the Lord.

4 Marching with thy Cross their banner,
  They have triumphed following
Thee, the Captain of salvation,
  Thee their Saviour and their King ;
Gladly, Lord, with thee they suffered ;
  Gladly, Lord, with thee they died,
And by death to life immortal
  They were born, and glorified.

5 Now they reign in heavenly glory,
  Now they walk in golden light,
Now they drink, as from a river,
  Holy bliss and infinite,
Love and peace they taste for ever,
  And all truth and knowledge see
In the beatific vision
  Of the blessèd Trinity.

6. God of God, the One-begotten,
  Light of light, Emmanuel,
In whose Body joined together
  All the Saints for ever dwell,
Pour upon us of thy fullness,
  That we may for evermore
God the Father, God the Son, and
  God the Holy Ghost adore.

A-men.

26

(Holy Communion)

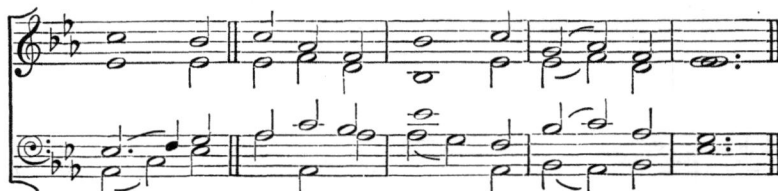

Bishop Reginald Heber, 1783–1826.

BREAD of the world in mercy broken,
Wine of the soul in mercy shed,
By whom the words of life were spoken,
And in whose death our sins are dead,
Look on the heart by sorrow broken,
Look on the tears by sinners shed,
And be thy feast to us the token
That by thy grace our souls are fed.

A-men.

If this hymn is sung during the Office of Holy Communion, it is suggested that it be sung thrice, with brief pauses intervening; first as a solo, then as an unaccompanied motet, and lastly with accompaniment.

INDEX OF FIRST LINES

The references are to 'The English Hymnal' (Oxford University Press), 'Hymns Ancient and Modern' (William Clowes & Sons), and 'The Church Hymnary' (Oxford University Press).

<u>Discographies by Travis & Emery:</u>

<u>Discographies by John Hunt.</u>

1987: From Adam to Webern: the Recordings of von Karajan.

1991: 3 Italian Conductors and 7 Viennese Sopranos: 10 Discographies: Arturo Toscanini, Guido Cantelli, Carlo Maria Giulini, Elisabeth Schwarzkopf, Irmgard Seefried, Elisabeth Gruemmer, Sena Jurinac, Hilde Gueden, Lisa Della Casa, Rita Streich.

1992: Mid-Century Conductors and More Viennese Singers: 10 Discographies: Karl Boehm, Victor De Sabata, Hans Knappertsbusch, Tullio Serafin, Clemens Krauss, Anton Dermota, Leonie Rysanek, Eberhard Waechter, Maria Reining, Erich Kunz.

1993: More 20th Century Conductors: 7 Discographies: Eugen Jochum, Ferenc Fricsay, Carl Schuricht, Felix Weingartner, Josef Krips, Otto Klemperer, Erich Kleiber.

1994: Giants of the Keyboard: 6 Discographies: Wilhelm Kempff, Walter Gieseking, Edwin Fischer, Clara Haskil, Wilhelm Backhaus, Artur Schnabel.

1994: Six Wagnerian Sopranos: 6 Discographies: Frieda Leider, Kirsten Flagstad, Astrid Varnay, Martha Moedl, Birgit Nilsson, Gwyneth Jones.

1995: Musical Knights: 6 Discographies: Henry Wood, Thomas Beecham, Adrian Boult, John Barbirolli, Reginald Goodall, Malcolm Sargent.

1995: A Notable Quartet: 4 Discographies: Gundula Janowitz, Christa Ludwig, Nicolai Gedda, Dietrich Fischer-Dieskau.

1996: The Post-War German Tradition: 5 Discographies: Rudolf Kempe, Joseph Keilberth, Wolfgang Sawallisch, Rafael Kubelik, Andre Cluytens.

1996: Teachers and Pupils: 7 Discographies: Elisabeth Schwarzkopf, Maria Ivoguen, Maria Cebotari, Meta Seinemeyer, Ljuba Welitsch, Rita Streich, Erna Berger.

1996: Tenors in a Lyric Tradition: 3 Discographies: Peter Anders, Walther Ludwig, Fritz Wunderlich.

1997: The Lyric Baritone: 5 Discographies: Hans Reinmar, Gerhard Hüsch, Josef Metternich, Hermann Uhde, Eberhard Wächter.

1997: Hungarians in Exile: 3 Discographies: Fritz Reiner, Antal Dorati, George Szell.

1997: The Art of the Diva: 3 Discographies: Claudia Muzio, Maria Callas, Magda Olivero.

1997: Metropolitan Sopranos: 4 Discographies: Rosa Ponselle, Eleanor Steber, Zinka Milanov, Leontyne Price.

1997: Back From The Shadows: 4 Discographies: Willem Mengelberg, Dimitri Mitropoulos, Hermann Abendroth, Eduard Van Beinum.

1997: More Musical Knights: 4 Discographies: Hamilton Harty, Charles Mackerras, Simon Rattle, John Pritchard.

1998: Conductors On The Yellow Label: 8 Discographies: Fritz Lehmann, Ferdinand Leitner, Ferenc Fricsay, Eugen Jochum, Leopold Ludwig, Artur Rother, Franz Konwitschny, Igor Markevitch.

1998: More Giants of the Keyboard: 5 Discographies: Claudio Arrau, Gyorgy Cziffra, Vladimir Horowitz, Dinu Lipatti, Artur Rubinstein.

1998: Mezzos and Contraltos: 5 Discographies: Janet Baker, Margarete Klose, Kathleen Ferrier, Giulietta Simionato, Elisabeth Höngen.

1999: The Furtwängler Sound Sixth Edition: Discography and Concert Listing.

1999: The Great Dictators: 3 Discographies: Evgeny Mravinsky, Artur Rodzinski, Sergiu Celibidache.

1999: Sviatoslav Richter: Pianist of the Century: Discography.

2000: Philharmonic Autocrat 1: Discography of: Herbert Von Karajan [Third Edition].

2000: Wiener Philharmoniker 1 - Vienna Philharmonic & Vienna State Opera Orchestras: Disc. Part 1 1905-1954.

2000: Wiener Philharmoniker 2 - Vienna Philharmonic & Vienna State Opera Orchestras: Disc. Part 2 1954-1989.

2001: Gramophone Stalwarts: 3 Separate Discographies: Bruno Walter, Erich Leinsdorf, Georg Solti.

2001: Singers of the Third Reich: 5 Discographies: Helge Roswaenge, Tiana Lemnitz, Franz Völker, Maria Müller, Max Lorenz.

2001: Philharmonic Autocrat 2: Concert Register of Herbert Von Karajan Second Edition.

2002: Sächsische Staatskapelle Dresden: Complete Discography.

2002: Carlo Maria Giulini: Discography and Concert Register.

2002: Pianists For The Connoisseur: 6 Discographies: Arturo Benedetti Michelangeli, Alfred Cortot, Alexis Weissenberg, Clifford Curzon, Solomon, Elly Ney.

2003: Singers on the Yellow Label: 7 Discographies: Maria Stader, Elfriede Trötschel, Annelies Kupper, Wolfgang Windgassen, Ernst Häfliger, Josef Greindl, Kim Borg.

2003: A Gallic Trio: 3 Discographies: Charles Münch, Paul Paray, Pierre Monteux.

2004: Antal Dorati 1906-1988: Discography and Concert Register.

2004: Columbia 33CX Label Discography.

2004: Great Violinists: 3 Discographies: David Oistrakh, Wolfgang Schneiderhan, Arthur Grumiaux.

2006: Leopold Stokowski: Second Edition of the Discography.

2006: Wagner Im Festspielhaus: Discography of the Bayreuth Festival.

2006: Her Master's Voice: Concert Register and Discography of Dame Elisabeth Schwarzkopf [Third Edition].

2007: Hans Knappertsbusch: Kna: Concert Register and Discography of Hans Knappertsbusch, 1888-1965. Second Edition.

2008: Philips Minigroove: Second Extended Version of the European Discography.

2009: American Classics: The Discographies of Leonard Bernstein and Eugene Ormandy.

Discography by Stephen J. Pettitt, edited by John Hunt:
1987: Philharmonia Orchestra: Complete Discography 1945-1987

Available from: Travis & Emery at 17 Cecil Court, London, UK. (+44) 20 7 240 2129. email on sales@travis-and-emery.com .

Music and Books published by Travis & Emery Music Bookshop:

Anon.: Hymnarium Sarisburense, cum Rubris et Notis Musicus
Agricola, Johann Friedrich from Tosi: Anleitung zur Singkunst. (Faksimile 1757)
Bach, C.P.E.: edited W. Emery: Nekrolog or Obituary Notice of J.S. Bach.
Bateson, Naomi Judith: Alcock of Salisbury
Bathe, William: A Briefe Introduction to the Skill of Song
Bax, Arnold: Symphony #5, Arranged for Piano Four Hands by Walter Emery
Burney, Charles: The Present State of Music in France and Italy
Burney, Charles: The Present State of Music in Germany, The Netherlands ...
Burney, Charles: An Account of the Musical Performances ... Handel
Burney, Karl: Nachricht von Georg Friedrich Handel's Lebensumstanden.
Burns, Robert (jnr): The Caledonian Musical Museum (1810 volume)
Cobbett, W.W.: Cobbett's Cyclopedic Survey of Chamber Music. (2 vols.)
Corrette, Michel: Le Maitre de Clavecin
Crimp, Bryan: Dear Mr. Rosenthal ... Dear Mr. Gaisberg ...
Crimp, Bryan: Solo: The Biography of Solomon
d'Indy, Vincent: Beethoven: Biographie Critique
d'Indy, Vincent: Beethoven: A Critical Biography
d'Indy, Vincent: César Franck (in French)
Fischhof, Joseph: Versuch einer Geschichte des Clavierbaues
Frescobaldi, Girolamo: D'Arie Musicali per Cantarsi. Primo Libro & Secondo Libro.
Geminiani, Francesco: The Art of Playing the Violin.
Handel; Purcell; Boyce; Green et al: Calliope or English Harmony: Volume First.
Hawkins, John: A General History of the Science and Practice of Music (5 vols.)
Herbert-Caesari, Edgar: The Science and Sensations of Vocal Tone
Herbert-Caesari, Edgar: Vocal Truth
Hopkins and Rimboult: The Organ. Its History and Construction.
Hunt, John: some 40 discographies – see list of discographies
Isaacs, Lewis: Hänsel and Gretel. A Guide to Humperdinck's Opera.
Isaacs, Lewis: Königskinder (Royal Children) A Guide to Humperdinck's Opera.
Lacassagne, M. l'Abbé Joseph : Traité Général des élémens du Chant.
Lascelles (née Catley), Anne: The Life of Miss Anne Catley.
Mainwaring, John: Memoirs of the Life of the Late George Frederic Handel
Malcolm, Alexander: A Treaty of Music: Speculative, Practical and Historical
Marx, Adolph Bernhard: Die Kunst des Gesanges, Theoretisch-Practisch
May, Florence: The Life of Brahms
Mellers, Wilfrid: Angels of the Night: Popular Female Singers of Our Time
Mellers, Wilfrid: Bach and the Dance of God

Travis & Emery Music Bookshop
17 Cecil Court, London, WC2N 4EZ, United Kingdom.
Tel. (+44) 20 7240 2129

Music and Books published by Travis & Emery Music Bookshop:

Mellers, Wilfrid: Beethoven and the Voice of God
Mellers, Wilfrid: Caliban Reborn - Renewal in Twentieth Century Music
Mellers, Wilfrid: François Couperin and the French Classical Tradition
Mellers, Wilfrid: Harmonious Meeting
Mellers, Wilfrid: Le Jardin Retrouvé, The Music of Frederic Mompou
Mellers, Wilfrid: Music and Society, England and the European Tradition
Mellers, Wilfrid: Music in a New Found Land: ... ... American Music
Mellers, Wilfrid: Romanticism and the Twentieth Century (from 1800)
Mellers, Wilfrid: The Masks of Orpheus: ...... the Story of European Music.
Mellers, Wilfrid: The Sonata Principle (from c. 1750)
Mellers, Wilfrid: Vaughan Williams and the Vision of Albion
Panchianio, Cattuffio: Rutzvanscad Il Giovine.
Pearce, Charles: Sims Reeves, Fifty Years of Music in England.
Pettitt, Stephen: Philharmonia Orchestra: Complete Discography 1945-1987
Playford, John: An Introduction to the Skill of Musick.
Purcell, Henry et al: Harmonia Sacra ... The First Book, (1726)
Purcell, Henry et al: Harmonia Sacra ... Book II (1726)
Quantz, Johann: Versuch einer Anweisung die Flöte traversiere zu spielen.
Rameau, Jean-Philippe: Code de Musique Pratique, ou Méthodes.
Rastall, Richard: The Notation of Western Music.
Rimbault, Edward: The Pianoforte, Its Origins, Progress, and Construction.
Rousseau, Jean Jacques: Dictionnaire de Musique
Rubinstein, Anton : Guide to the proper use of the Pianoforte Pedals.
Sainsbury, John S.: Dictionary of Musicians. Vol. 1. (1825). 2 vols.
Simpson, Christopher: A Compendium of Practical Musick in Five Parts
Spohr, Louis: Autobiography
Spohr, Louis: Grand Violin School
Tans'ur, William: A New Musical Grammar; or The Harmonical Spectator
Terry, Charles Sanford: Four-Part Chorals of J.S. Bach. (German & English)
Terry, Charles Sanford: Joh. Seb. Bach, Cantata Texts, Sacred and Secular.
Terry, Charles Sanford: The Origins of the Family of Bach Musicians.
Tosi, Pierfrancesco: Opinioni de' Cantori Antichi, e Moderni
Van der Straeten, Edmund: History of the Violoncello, The Viol da Gamba ...
Van der Straeten, Edmund: History of the Violin, Its Ancestors... (2 vols.)
Walther, J. G.: Musicalisches Lexikon ober Musicalische Bibliothec (1732)

Travis & Emery Music Bookshop
17 Cecil Court, London, WC2N 4EZ, United Kingdom.
Tel. (+44) 20 7240 2129

www.ingramcontent.com/pod-product-compliance
Lightning Source LLC
Chambersburg PA
CBHW071423040426
42445CB00012BA/1277

* 9 781906 857349 *